"Unlocking the Secrets of Success:

Strategies from the World's Top Achievers"

"Discover the Habits, Mindsets, and Practices That Propel You Toward Success"

HUGO HUYER

Copyright © [2024] [HUGO HUYER]

All rights reserved. No part of this publication may be reproduced, distributed, or transmitted in any form or by any means, including photocopying, recording, or other electronic or mechanical methods, without the prior written permission of the publisher, except in the case of brief quotations embodied in critical reviews and certain other noncommercial uses permitted by copyright law.

The views expressed in this book are solely those of the author and do not necessarily reflect the views of the publisher or any affiliated individuals or organizations.

Table of Contents

Introduction 5
    Understanding Success: Defining the Path Ahead 6
    The Importance of Studying Top Achievers 7
    Overview of the Book's Structure 8

Foundations of Success 11
    Defining Success: What Does it Mean to You? 11
    Setting Clear Goals and Objectives 12
    Cultivating a Growth Mindset 13
    Developing Self-Discipline and Resilience 14
    Embracing Failure as a Stepping Stone to Success 15

Habits of Top Achievers 17
    Morning Routines: Starting Your Day Right 17
    The Power of Positive Thinking and Affirmations 18
    Effective Time Management Strategies 19
    Prioritization Techniques for Maximum Productivity 20
    Consistency: The Key to Sustainable Success 21
    Building Healthy Habits for Physical and Mental Well-being** 22

Mindsets for Success 24
    Adopting an Abundance Mentality 24
    Overcoming Limiting Beliefs and Fears 25
    Maintaining a Positive Attitude in the Face of Challenges 26

Harnessing the Power of Visualization and Manifestation 27
    Cultivating a Sense of Gratitude and Appreciation 28

Strategies for Professional Success 30
    Networking and Relationship Building 30
    Effective Communication Skills 31
    Negotiation Tactics and Conflict Resolution 32
    Leadership Principles for Success 33

- Continuous Learning and Skill Development 34
- Financial Success Strategies 36
  - Financial Planning and Goal Setting 36
  - Investing Wisely: Strategies from Successful Investors 37
  - Building Multiple Streams of Income 38
  - Budgeting and Managing Finances Effectively 39
- Balancing Success with Well-being 41
  - Avoiding Burnout: Strategies for Work-Life Balance 41
  - The Importance of Rest and Relaxation 42
  - Mindfulness and Stress Management Techniques 43
  - Nurturing Relationships and Social Connections 44
- Case Studies of Success 46
  - Profiles of Top Achievers from Various Fields 46
  - Analysis of Their Habits, Mindsets, and Strategies 47
  - Lessons Learned and Takeaways for Readers 49
- Putting it All Together: Your Personal Success Plan 51
  - Reflecting on Your Goals and Aspirations 51
  - Creating a Customized Success Blueprint 52
  - Implementing Strategies and Tracking Progress 52
  - Adjusting and Iterating for Continuous Improvement 53
- Conclusion 55
  - Recap of Key Insights and Lessons 55
  - Final Thoughts on the Journey Ahead 57
- References 59

Introduction

Success. It's a word that resonates deeply within us all. It's the fuel that ignites our ambitions, the beacon guiding us through the stormy seas of uncertainty, and the ultimate destination of our dreams. Yet, despite its universal allure, success remains an enigma to many. What is the secret formula that separates the highly successful from the rest of us? How do some individuals seemingly effortlessly ascend to the pinnacle of achievement while others struggle to make even a modest dent in the universe?

In this journey of exploration, we embark on a quest to unravel the mysteries of success. We delve into the lives of the world's top achievers, dissecting their habits, scrutinizing their mindsets, and uncovering the strategies that propel them forward. Welcome to "Unlocking the Secrets of Success: Strategies from the World's Top Achievers.

Understanding Success: Defining the Path Ahead

Before we set sail on this voyage, it's imperative that we first define our destination. What exactly is success? Is it measured solely by wealth and fame, or does it encompass a broader spectrum of achievements and fulfillment? Success, in its truest essence, transcends mere material possessions or societal acclaim. It encompasses a holistic harmony between one's professional endeavors, personal growth, and contribution to the greater good.

For some, success may manifest as financial prosperity, the ability to provide for oneself and loved ones, and the freedom to pursue passions without the constraints of financial worry. For others, it may take the form of creative expression, leaving an indelible mark on the world through art, music, literature, or innovation. Still, for others, success may be found in the realm of relationships, fostering meaningful connections, and leaving a positive impact on the lives of others.

However, irrespective of the myriad manifestations of success, there exists a common thread that binds them all: the relentless pursuit of excellence, fueled by passion, purpose, and perseverance. It is this unwavering commitment to self-improvement and the relentless pursuit of one's dreams that sets the stage for extraordinary achievement.

The Importance of Studying Top Achievers

In our quest for success, there is no better guide than those who have already traversed the path we aspire to tread. The world's top achievers serve as beacons of inspiration, illuminating the way forward with their remarkable stories of triumph over adversity, unwavering determination, and unwavering commitment to their dreams.

By studying the habits, mindsets, and practices of these exceptional individuals, we gain invaluable insights into the principles and strategies that underpin their success. We uncover the rituals they adhere to, the beliefs they hold dear, and the actions they take consistently to propel themselves toward their goals.

Moreover, the stories of top achievers remind us that success is not the exclusive domain of the privileged few but is attainable by anyone willing to put in the effort, dedication, and resilience required to overcome obstacles and seize opportunities.

Overview of the Book's Structure

Now that we have laid the groundwork for our exploration of success, let us take a moment to survey the terrain ahead. "Unlocking the Secrets of Success" is structured as a comprehensive roadmap, guiding you through the various dimensions of achievement and providing actionable insights and strategies along the way.

In the following chapters, we will delve into the foundational principles of success, exploring the importance of goal setting, cultivating a growth mindset, and developing the self-discipline and resilience necessary to weather the storms of adversity. We will then examine the habits of top achievers, uncovering the morning routines, positive thinking practices, and time management strategies that set them apart.

Next, we will explore the mindsets that underpin success, discussing the importance of adopting an abundance mentality, overcoming limiting beliefs, and maintaining a positive attitude in the face of challenges. We will then turn our attention to strategies for professional success, delving into the nuances of networking, communication, leadership, and continuous learning.

Additionally, we will explore the role of financial success in achieving overall fulfillment, discussing the importance of financial planning, investing wisely, and building multiple streams of income. We will also examine the delicate balance between success and well-being, discussing strategies for avoiding burnout, managing stress, and nurturing relationships.

Throughout our journey, we will draw upon the wisdom of top achievers from various fields, analyzing their stories, and distilling actionable insights that you can apply to your own life. Finally, we will provide you with practical tools and frameworks for creating your personalized success plan, empowering you to chart your course toward the life of your dreams.

So, dear reader, prepare to embark on a transformative journey of discovery and empowerment. The path to success awaits, and with the insights and strategies contained within these pages, you possess the keys to unlock its secrets. Let us begin.

Foundations of Success

Success is not merely a destination; it is a journey, a process, and a state of being. It is the culmination of deliberate actions, aligned with a clear vision and driven by unwavering determination. In this section, we delve into the foundational principles that underpin success, exploring the fundamental concepts and practices that serve as the bedrock upon which achievement is built.

DEFINING SUCCESS: WHAT DOES IT MEAN TO YOU?

At the heart of every successful endeavor lies a clear and compelling vision of what success looks like. Yet, defining success is a deeply personal and subjective endeavor, shaped by our unique values, aspirations, and life experiences. For some, success may entail climbing the corporate ladder, attaining wealth and status, or achieving recognition in their chosen field. For others, it may involve cultivating deep and meaningful relationships, making a positive impact on the lives of others, or pursuing creative endeavors that bring joy and fulfillment.

Regardless of the specific form it takes, the key to defining success lies in introspection and self-awareness. It requires us to reflect deeply on our values, passions, and long-term aspirations, and to align our goals and actions accordingly. By clarifying what success means to us personally, we lay the groundwork for a journey that is both purposeful and fulfilling.

Setting Clear Goals and Objectives

Once we have defined our vision of success, the next step is to translate it into tangible goals and objectives. Goals provide us with a roadmap for our journey, guiding our actions and decisions in a purposeful direction. They serve as beacons of light, illuminating the path ahead and motivating us to stay focused and disciplined in the pursuit of our dreams.

Effective goal setting involves several key principles. First and foremost, goals should be specific, measurable, achievable, relevant, and time-bound (SMART). By articulating our goals in clear and concrete terms, we enhance our clarity and commitment, making it easier to track our progress and stay accountable.

Moreover, goals should be aligned with our values, passions, and long-term vision of success. They should stretch us beyond our comfort zones, inspiring us to reach for new heights while remaining within the realm of feasibility. By setting goals that are both challenging and attainable, we cultivate a sense of purpose and momentum that propels us forward on our journey.

CULTIVATING A GROWTH MINDSET

Central to the pursuit of success is the cultivation of a growth mindset – a belief in our ability to learn, grow, and adapt in the face of challenges. Unlike a fixed mindset, which views abilities as innate and unchangeable, a growth mindset sees setbacks and failures as opportunities for growth and learning. It thrives on challenge, embraces effort, and celebrates progress, recognizing that mastery is not the result of innate talent but of persistent practice and resilience.

Cultivating a growth mindset involves challenging our limiting beliefs, reframing failures as learning experiences, and embracing the power of "yet" – the belief that our abilities can be developed over time with dedication and effort. By adopting a growth mindset, we unlock our full potential and open ourselves up to a world of possibilities, where obstacles become stepping stones to success and setbacks become opportunities for growth.

DEVELOPING SELF-DISCIPLINE AND RESILIENCE

Success rarely comes easy. It requires discipline, perseverance, and the ability to overcome obstacles and setbacks along the way. Developing self-discipline is essential for staying focused and motivated in the pursuit of our goals, resisting distractions, and staying committed to our priorities even when the going gets tough.

Self-discipline is not about depriving ourselves of pleasure or forcing ourselves to endure hardship; rather, it is about cultivating habits and routines that support our long-term goals and aspirations. It involves setting clear boundaries, managing our time effectively, and prioritizing tasks based on their importance and urgency.

Similarly, resilience – the ability to bounce back from adversity – is a critical skill for success. Resilient individuals are able to weather the storms of life with grace and fortitude, bouncing back stronger and more resilient than before. They view setbacks not as failures but as temporary setbacks, opportunities for growth and self-discovery.

Embracing Failure as a Stepping Stone to Success

In the pursuit of success, failure is not the opposite of success; it is an integral part of the journey. Every setback, every obstacle, and every defeat is an opportunity for growth and learning, a chance to refine our approach, and a stepping stone on the path to success.

Embracing failure requires us to shift our perspective and reframe setbacks as valuable learning experiences. Rather than dwelling on our mistakes or allowing them to demoralize us, we can choose to extract lessons from them, adapting our strategies and approaches based on what we have learned.

Failure teaches us resilience, perseverance, and humility – qualities that are essential for success in any endeavor. It reminds us that success is not a straight line but a winding road, filled with twists and turns, ups and downs. By embracing failure as a natural part of the journey, we free ourselves from the fear of failure and empower ourselves to take risks, pursue our passions, and ultimately achieve our goals.

Habits of Top Achievers

In the pursuit of success, our daily habits play a pivotal role in shaping our outcomes. Top achievers understand the power of consistency and discipline in their routines, cultivating habits that fuel their productivity, creativity, and overall well-being. In this section, we explore the key habits practiced by the world's top achievers and how you can incorporate them into your own life to unlock your full potential.

Morning Routines: Starting Your Day Right

The way we start our day sets the tone for the rest of our waking hours. Top achievers recognize the importance of a well-crafted morning routine in optimizing their productivity and mental clarity. Whether it's waking up early to seize the day, engaging in meditation or mindfulness practices to center themselves, or indulging in physical exercise to energize their bodies, morning routines serve as the launching pad for a day of success.

By establishing a consistent morning routine tailored to your unique needs and preferences, you can cultivate a sense of purpose and momentum that propels you forward throughout the day. Whether it's journaling, setting intentions for the day ahead, or fueling your body with nutritious foods, starting your day right lays the foundation for a day filled with focus, productivity, and fulfillment.

The Power of Positive Thinking and Affirmations

Our thoughts have a profound impact on our emotions, behaviors, and ultimately, our outcomes in life. Top achievers harness the power of positive thinking and affirmations to cultivate a mindset of abundance, optimism, and resilience. They recognize that the way we perceive ourselves and our circumstances shapes our reality, and they consciously choose to focus on thoughts and beliefs that empower and uplift them.

Affirmations are powerful tools for reprogramming the subconscious mind, replacing limiting beliefs with empowering ones and aligning our thoughts and actions with our goals and aspirations. By regularly affirming our worth, capabilities, and potential for success, we can overcome self-doubt, fear, and negative self-talk, and unlock our innate potential to achieve greatness.

EFFECTIVE TIME MANAGEMENT STRATEGIES

Time is our most precious resource, yet it is also finite and nonrenewable. Top achievers understand the importance of effective time management in maximizing their productivity and achieving their goals. They prioritize tasks based on their importance and urgency, set clear boundaries to minimize distractions, and allocate their time and energy wisely to activities that align with their priorities and long-term objectives.

Effective time management involves several key principles, including setting specific goals and deadlines, breaking tasks down into manageable chunks, and leveraging tools and techniques such as time blocking and the Pomodoro Technique to enhance focus and concentration. By mastering the art of time management, you can optimize your productivity, minimize procrastination, and create space for the activities and experiences that matter most to you.

PRIORITIZATION TECHNIQUES FOR MAXIMUM PRODUCTIVITY

In a world filled with competing demands and distractions, the ability to prioritize effectively is essential for success. Top achievers employ various prioritization techniques to identify and focus on tasks that yield the greatest impact and value. Whether it's using the Eisenhower Matrix to distinguish between urgent and important tasks, the ABCDE method to rank tasks based on their priority, or the Pareto Principle to focus on the 20% of activities that yield 80% of results, prioritization enables them to make informed decisions about how to allocate their time and resources.

By adopting a systematic approach to prioritization, you can avoid the trap of busyness and ensure that your efforts are aligned with your overarching goals and objectives. Whether it's setting daily, weekly, or monthly priorities, regularly reviewing and adjusting your plans as needed, or delegating tasks that fall outside your area of expertise, effective prioritization enables you to work smarter, not harder, and achieve greater results with less effort.

Consistency: The Key to Sustainable Success

Consistency is the hallmark of all great achievements. It is the steady accumulation of small actions taken consistently over time that leads to extraordinary results. Top achievers understand the power of consistency in achieving their goals, and they commit themselves to showing up every day, regardless of the obstacles or setbacks they may face.

Consistency involves developing habits and routines that support our long-term goals and aspirations, whether it's practicing a skill daily, writing a certain number of words each day, or exercising regularly to maintain physical and mental well-being. By showing up consistently and putting in the work day in and day out, we build momentum, cultivate resilience, and ultimately, achieve success that is both sustainable and fulfilling.

Building Healthy Habits for Physical and Mental Well-being**

Success is not just about achieving external accolades or material wealth; it is also about nurturing our physical and mental well-being. Top achievers prioritize self-care and cultivate habits that support their overall health and vitality. Whether it's getting an adequate amount of sleep each night, fueling their bodies with nutritious foods, or engaging in regular exercise to stay fit and energized, they understand that a healthy body is the foundation for a successful life.

Moreover, top achievers prioritize their mental well-being, practicing mindfulness, meditation, or other stress-reduction techniques to cultivate a sense of inner peace and balance. They recognize the importance of taking regular breaks, disconnecting from technology, and spending time in nature to recharge and rejuvenate their minds and spirits.

By building healthy habits for physical and mental well-being, you can enhance your resilience, creativity, and overall quality of life. Whether it's incorporating relaxation techniques into your daily routine, seeking support from friends and loved ones, or prioritizing activities that bring you joy and fulfillment, investing in your well-being is essential for long-term success and happiness.

Mindsets for Success

Success is not solely determined by external factors or circumstances; it is equally influenced by our internal beliefs, attitudes, and mindsets. In this section, we explore the transformative power of mindset in shaping our outcomes and unlocking our full potential. From adopting an abundance mentality to cultivating a sense of gratitude and appreciation, these mindsets serve as the foundation for a life of purpose, fulfillment, and achievement.

Adopting an Abundance Mentality

At the heart of abundance mentality lies the belief that there is more than enough to go around – enough opportunities, resources, and success for everyone. Unlike a scarcity mindset, which views life as a zero-sum game characterized by competition and scarcity, an abundance mentality sees the world as a place of limitless possibilities and potential.

By adopting an abundance mentality, we shift our focus from scarcity and lack to abundance and opportunity. We embrace the belief that success is not finite but infinite, and that there is room for everyone to thrive and succeed. This mindset empowers us to celebrate the success of others, collaborate rather than compete, and approach challenges with a sense of optimism and possibility.

OVERCOMING LIMITING BELIEFS AND FEARS

Our beliefs shape our reality, often more profoundly than we realize. Limiting beliefs – deeply ingrained convictions about our abilities, worthiness, and potential – can hold us back from pursuing our dreams and achieving our goals. Similarly, fears – whether of failure, rejection, or inadequacy – can paralyze us and prevent us from taking the necessary risks to grow and succeed.

Overcoming limiting beliefs and fears requires courage, self-awareness, and a willingness to challenge our assumptions about ourselves and the world around us. It involves questioning the validity of our beliefs, reframing negative thoughts, and replacing them with empowering ones. Moreover, it requires us to confront our fears head-on, taking gradual steps outside our comfort zones and building resilience in the face of adversity.

Maintaining a Positive Attitude in the Face of Challenges

Success is not immune to setbacks, obstacles, and failures; indeed, they are an inevitable part of the journey. What sets successful individuals apart is not the absence of challenges but their response to them. Maintaining a positive attitude in the face of challenges is essential for overcoming adversity, staying resilient, and ultimately, achieving our goals.

A positive attitude is not about denying the existence of problems or minimizing their impact; rather, it is about approaching them with optimism, resilience, and a sense of possibility. It involves reframing setbacks as opportunities for growth, focusing on solutions rather than dwelling on problems, and maintaining faith in our ability to overcome obstacles and persevere in the pursuit of our dreams.

Harnessing the Power of Visualization and Manifestation

Visualization is a powerful tool for manifesting our desires and bringing our goals to fruition. By vividly imagining ourselves achieving our goals, we activate the creative power of our minds and align our thoughts and actions with our desired outcomes. Visualization involves engaging all of our senses to create a rich and immersive mental picture of our success, allowing us to experience it as if it were already a reality.

Moreover, visualization is not merely a passive exercise but a proactive one; it involves taking inspired action toward our goals and leveraging the power of intention to bring them into manifestation. By combining visualization with deliberate action, we create a powerful synergy that accelerates our progress and propels us toward our dreams with greater speed and certainty.

Cultivating a Sense of Gratitude and Appreciation

Gratitude is the antidote to scarcity and dissatisfaction; it is the key to unlocking abundance and fulfillment in our lives. Cultivating a sense of gratitude and appreciation involves acknowledging and savoring the blessings, big and small, that enrich our lives each day – from the beauty of nature to the kindness of strangers, from the love of family and friends to the opportunities that come our way.

Gratitude shifts our focus from what we lack to what we have, from scarcity to abundance, and from complaint to contentment. It imbues us with a sense of humility and awe, reminding us of the interconnectedness of all things and the inherent goodness of life. Moreover, gratitude is a practice that can be cultivated and nurtured over time, through simple rituals such as keeping a gratitude journal, expressing appreciation to others, or taking a moment each day to count our blessings.

By cultivating a mindset of abundance, overcoming limiting beliefs and fears, maintaining a positive attitude in the face of challenges, harnessing the power of visualization and manifestation, and cultivating a sense of gratitude and appreciation, we can unlock our full potential and create a life of purpose, fulfillment, and success.

Strategies for Professional Success

Achieving success in the professional realm requires more than just talent and hard work; it demands a strategic approach to navigating the complexities of the modern workplace. In this section, we delve into the essential strategies for professional success, from cultivating strong relationships to honing effective communication skills, mastering negotiation tactics, embracing leadership principles, and committing to continuous learning and skill development.

Networking and Relationship Building

In the interconnected world of business, success often hinges on the strength of our relationships and our ability to cultivate a robust network of contacts. Networking is not merely about exchanging business cards or attending events; it is about building genuine connections based on trust, mutual respect, and shared interests.

Effective networking involves cultivating relationships both within and outside our immediate circles, seeking out opportunities to connect with peers, mentors, industry leaders, and potential collaborators. It requires active listening, genuine curiosity, and a willingness to offer value and support to others without expecting immediate returns.

By investing time and effort into nurturing our professional relationships, we can expand our opportunities, gain valuable insights and perspectives, and access resources and opportunities that may otherwise be out of reach.

EFFECTIVE COMMUNICATION SKILLS

Effective communication is the cornerstone of success in any professional setting. Whether it's articulating ideas persuasively, delivering compelling presentations, or navigating difficult conversations with grace and diplomacy, strong communication skills are essential for building trust, fostering collaboration, and achieving our goals.

Effective communication involves not only conveying our message clearly and concisely but also actively listening to others, seeking to understand their perspectives, and responding thoughtfully and empathetically. It requires awareness of verbal and nonverbal cues, adaptability in our communication style, and a commitment to clarity and transparency.

By honing our communication skills, we can enhance our influence, build stronger relationships, and navigate the complexities of the workplace with greater confidence and effectiveness.

NEGOTIATION TACTICS AND CONFLICT RESOLUTION

Negotiation is an essential skill for success in the professional world, whether it's securing a higher salary, closing a deal, or resolving conflicts with colleagues or clients. Effective negotiation involves understanding the interests and motivations of all parties involved, identifying common ground, and finding mutually beneficial solutions to complex problems.

Key negotiation tactics include active listening, asking probing questions, and reframing issues to find creative win-win solutions. Conflict resolution, on the other hand, requires patience, empathy, and a willingness to seek common ground while addressing the underlying issues causing the conflict.

By mastering negotiation tactics and conflict resolution strategies, we can navigate professional challenges with confidence, build consensus, and achieve outcomes that satisfy all parties involved.

LEADERSHIP PRINCIPLES FOR SUCCESS

Effective leadership is not about wielding power or authority; it's about inspiring others to reach their full potential and achieve shared goals. Whether leading a team, a project, or an entire organization, successful leaders embody certain principles and values that set them apart.

Key leadership principles include leading by example, empowering others, fostering a culture of collaboration and innovation, and cultivating emotional intelligence and empathy. Successful leaders are visionaries who can articulate a compelling vision, motivate and inspire others to work toward it, and adapt to changing circumstances with grace and resilience.

By embracing leadership principles for success, we can unlock our potential as leaders, inspire those around us, and drive positive change within our organizations and communities.

Continuous Learning and Skill Development

In today's rapidly evolving business landscape, success demands a commitment to continuous learning and skill development. Whether it's staying abreast of industry trends, acquiring new technical skills, or honing leadership capabilities, successful professionals understand the importance of lifelong learning in maintaining their competitive edge.

Continuous learning involves seeking out opportunities for growth, whether through formal education, professional development programs, or self-directed learning initiatives. It requires a growth mindset – a belief in our ability to learn and grow throughout our lives – and a willingness to step outside our comfort zones and embrace new challenges.

By committing to continuous learning and skill development, we can adapt to changing circumstances, seize new opportunities, and position ourselves for long-term success in our chosen fields.

Financial Success Strategies

Achieving financial success requires more than just earning a paycheck; it demands a strategic approach to managing and growing your wealth over time. In this section, we explore key strategies for financial success, from effective financial planning and goal setting to prudent investing, diversifying income streams, and mastering the art of budgeting and financial management.

FINANCIAL PLANNING AND GOAL SETTING

At the heart of financial success lies a well-crafted plan and clear, actionable goals. Financial planning involves assessing your current financial situation, defining your long-term objectives, and creating a roadmap for achieving them. Whether it's saving for retirement, purchasing a home, or starting a business, effective financial planning enables you to allocate your resources strategically and make informed decisions about your finances.

Key components of financial planning include setting SMART (Specific, Measurable, Achievable, Relevant, Time-bound) goals, creating a budget to track your income and expenses, establishing an emergency fund for unexpected expenses, and developing a savings and investment strategy tailored to your objectives and risk tolerance.

By setting clear financial goals and developing a plan to achieve them, you can take control of your finances, build wealth systematically, and create a secure financial future for yourself and your loved ones.

Investing Wisely: Strategies from Successful Investors

Investing is a fundamental aspect of wealth-building, enabling you to grow your assets and generate passive income over time. However, successful investing requires more than just picking stocks or mutual funds at random; it demands a disciplined approach based on thorough research, careful analysis, and a long-term perspective.

Successful investors employ various strategies to maximize their returns while minimizing risk, including diversification, asset allocation, and dollar-cost averaging. They also understand the importance of staying informed about market trends, economic indicators, and geopolitical events that may impact their investments.

Whether you're interested in stocks, bonds, real estate, or alternative investments, the key to successful investing lies in conducting thorough due diligence, staying disciplined in your approach, and avoiding emotional decision-making.

Building Multiple Streams of Income

Diversifying your income streams is a key strategy for achieving financial security and independence. Relying solely on a single source of income, such as a job or business, leaves you vulnerable to economic downturns, job loss, or other unforeseen events. By building multiple streams of income, you can create a more stable and resilient financial foundation, reducing your dependence on any one source of revenue.

Multiple streams of income can take various forms, including rental income from real estate investments, dividends from stocks and bonds, royalties from intellectual property, or income from a side hustle or freelance work. The key is to identify opportunities that align with your skills, interests, and resources and to diversify your income sources to minimize risk and maximize potential returns.

BUDGETING AND MANAGING FINANCES EFFECTIVELY

Budgeting is the cornerstone of financial management, enabling you to track your income and expenses, prioritize your spending, and achieve your financial goals. Effective budgeting involves creating a detailed plan for how you will allocate your resources, taking into account your income, expenses, debts, and savings goals.

Key components of effective budgeting include categorizing your expenses, identifying areas where you can reduce costs or eliminate unnecessary spending, and setting aside money for savings and investments. It also involves regularly reviewing and adjusting your budget as needed to reflect changes in your financial situation or goals.

In addition to budgeting, effective financial management requires staying organized, monitoring your cash flow, and being proactive about managing your debts and credit. By taking control of your finances and making informed decisions about how you allocate your resources, you can build wealth systematically and achieve financial freedom over time.

Balancing Success with Well-being.

Achieving success is not just about reaching the pinnacle of achievement in our professional or personal lives; it's also about maintaining a sense of well-being and fulfillment along the way. In this section, we explore strategies for balancing success with well-being, from avoiding burnout and cultivating work-life balance to prioritizing rest and relaxation, managing stress, and nurturing meaningful relationships and social connections.

AVOIDING BURNOUT: STRATEGIES FOR WORK-LIFE BALANCE

In today's fast-paced and demanding world, burnout has become increasingly common among high achievers. Burnout is a state of physical, mental, and emotional exhaustion caused by prolonged stress and overwork, and it can have serious consequences for our health, relationships, and overall well-being.

To avoid burnout, it's essential to prioritize work-life balance and set boundaries between our professional and personal lives. This may involve establishing clear work hours, taking regular breaks throughout the day, and disconnecting from work during evenings and weekends. It also involves identifying activities outside of work that bring us joy and fulfillment and making time for them regularly.

By prioritizing work-life balance and taking proactive steps to prevent burnout, we can preserve our energy and enthusiasm for our pursuits, leading to greater productivity, creativity, and overall well-being.

THE IMPORTANCE OF REST AND RELAXATION

Rest and relaxation are essential for recharging our batteries, replenishing our energy reserves, and maintaining optimal physical and mental health. Yet, in our culture of constant busyness and productivity, many of us neglect to prioritize rest and relaxation, viewing them as luxuries rather than necessities.

However, rest and relaxation are not indulgences; they are essential components of a balanced and fulfilling life. Whether it's getting an adequate amount of sleep each night, taking regular breaks throughout the day, or engaging in activities that promote relaxation and stress relief, such as meditation, yoga, or spending time in nature, prioritizing rest and relaxation is essential for maintaining our overall well-being.

By making time for rest and relaxation in our daily lives, we can reduce stress, improve our mood and cognitive function, and enhance our resilience in the face of challenges.

Mindfulness and Stress Management Techniques

Mindfulness is the practice of being fully present in the moment, without judgment or attachment. It involves paying attention to our thoughts, feelings, and bodily sensations with openness and curiosity, rather than reacting impulsively or automatically. Mindfulness has been shown to reduce stress, anxiety, and depression, and improve overall well-being.

Stress management techniques such as deep breathing, progressive muscle relaxation, and guided imagery can also help reduce stress and promote relaxation. These techniques work by activating the body's relaxation response, counteracting the effects of the stress response, and promoting a state of calm and tranquility.

By incorporating mindfulness and stress management techniques into our daily routine, we can cultivate greater awareness, resilience, and well-being, even in the face of life's challenges and uncertainties.

Nurturing Relationships and Social Connections

Human beings are social creatures by nature, and our relationships with others play a crucial role in our overall well-being and happiness. Nurturing meaningful relationships and social connections is essential for maintaining a sense of belonging, support, and connection in our lives.

This may involve spending quality time with friends and loved ones, reaching out to others for support and companionship, and participating in activities and groups that align with our interests and values. It also involves practicing empathy, active listening, and effective communication skills in our interactions with others, fostering deeper connections and understanding.

By prioritizing relationships and social connections in our lives, we can cultivate a support network that sustains us through life's ups and downs, enhances our sense of belonging and fulfillment, and contributes to our overall well-being and happiness.

Case Studies of Success

Examining the journeys of top achievers from various fields provides invaluable insights into the habits, mindsets, and strategies that contribute to their success. In this section, we present profiles of prominent individuals who have achieved remarkable success in their respective domains, analyze their habits and mindsets, and distill key lessons and takeaways for readers seeking to emulate their achievements.

PROFILES OF TOP ACHIEVERS FROM VARIOUS FIELDS

1. **Elon Musk** - Visionary entrepreneur and CEO of SpaceX, Tesla, and Neuralink. Musk's relentless pursuit of innovation and willingness to take bold risks have propelled him to the forefront of the technology and space industries.

2. **Oprah Winfrey** - Media mogul, philanthropist, and cultural icon. Winfrey's journey from a troubled childhood to global success serves as a testament to the power of resilience, authenticity, and perseverance.

3. **Warren Buffett** - Legendary investor and CEO of Berkshire Hathaway. Buffett's disciplined approach to investing, emphasis on value, and long-term perspective have made him one of the most successful investors of all time.

4. **Serena Williams** - Tennis champion and trailblazer. Williams's unmatched talent, relentless work ethic, and unwavering determination have propelled her to the pinnacle of her sport, inspiring generations of athletes around the world.

5. **Malala Yousafzai** - Nobel Prize laureate and advocate for girls' education. Yousafzai's courage, resilience, and unwavering commitment to social justice have made her a symbol of hope and inspiration for millions around the world.

Analysis of Their Habits, Mindsets, and Strategies

- ❖ **Vision and Goal Setting:** Top achievers like Musk and Winfrey demonstrate the importance of setting audacious goals and having a clear vision for the future.

They are relentless in their pursuit of excellence, constantly pushing the boundaries of what is possible.
- **Resilience and Perseverance:** Buffett, Williams, and Yousafzai exemplify resilience in the face of adversity. They have overcome numerous challenges and setbacks on their paths to success, demonstrating the importance of perseverance and determination in achieving one's goals.
- **Continuous Learning and Growth:** Successful individuals are lifelong learners who are constantly seeking new knowledge and skills. Buffett famously spends much of his day reading and learning, while Williams and Yousafzai are advocates for education and empowerment.
- **Risk-taking and Innovation:** Musk's willingness to take bold risks and pursue groundbreaking ideas has led to the creation of revolutionary companies like SpaceX and Tesla. Successful individuals understand that innovation often

requires stepping outside of one's comfort zone and embracing uncertainty.

LESSONS LEARNED AND TAKEAWAYS FOR READERS

- ❖ **Embrace Failure as a Learning Opportunity:** Each of the top achievers profiled in this section has experienced failure and setbacks along the way. However, they have not let these challenges define them or deter them from their goals. Instead, they have used failure as a catalyst for growth and innovation.
- ❖ **Stay True to Your Values and Purpose:** Winfrey and Yousafzai are examples of individuals who have remained true to their values and used their platforms to make a positive impact in the world. Successful individuals understand the importance of aligning their actions with their core beliefs and values.
- ❖ **Surround Yourself with a Strong Support Network:** Buffett and Musk credit much of their success to the mentors, partners, and colleagues who

have supported and guided them along the way. Building a strong support network is essential for navigating the challenges of entrepreneurship and achieving long-term success.

In studying the habits, mindsets, and strategies of these top achievers, readers can glean valuable insights and inspiration for their own journey toward success. By incorporating these lessons into their lives and careers, they can overcome obstacles, seize opportunities, and achieve their fullest potential.

Putting it All Together: Your Personal Success Plan

Achieving success is a journey that requires careful planning, deliberate action, and continuous refinement. In this section, we guide you through the process of creating your personalized success plan, incorporating the lessons and strategies discussed throughout this book to help you realize your goals and aspirations.

REFLECTING ON YOUR GOALS AND ASPIRATIONS

Begin by taking some time to reflect on your goals, aspirations, and values. What do you want to achieve in your personal and professional life? What are your deepest desires and dreams? Consider both short-term and long-term goals, and be specific about what success looks like for you in each area of your life.

Creating a Customized Success Blueprint

Once you have clarity on your goals and aspirations, it's time to create a customized success blueprint – a roadmap for achieving your objectives. Break down your goals into actionable steps, identifying the habits, mindsets, and strategies you need to cultivate to succeed. Consider how you can leverage your strengths, overcome your weaknesses, and capitalize on opportunities in your environment.

Your success blueprint should include specific goals, deadlines, and milestones to track your progress along the way. Be realistic about what you can accomplish within a given timeframe, and be prepared to adjust your plan as needed based on changing circumstances or feedback.

Implementing Strategies and Tracking Progress

With your success blueprint in hand, it's time to put your plan into action. Start by implementing the habits, mindsets, and strategies that align with your goals and aspirations. Whether it's setting aside time each day for focused work, practicing gratitude and mindfulness, or investing in your personal and professional development, commit to taking consistent action toward your goals.

Track your progress regularly, keeping a journal or using a goal-tracking app to monitor your successes and setbacks. Celebrate your wins along the way, no matter how small, and use any setbacks as opportunities for learning and growth. Stay focused on your long-term vision, and don't be afraid to course-correct if you veer off track.

Adjusting and Iterating for Continuous Improvement

Success is not a linear path; it's a journey filled with twists, turns, and unexpected detours. As you progress toward your goals, be prepared to adjust and iterate your plan based on new information or feedback. Stay open-minded and flexible, and be willing to experiment with new approaches or strategies if the ones you're using aren't yielding the desired results.

Seek feedback from mentors, peers, or trusted advisors, and use their insights to refine your approach and course-correct as needed. Remember that success is a lifelong journey, and that each step you take brings you closer to realizing your full potential.

By creating a personalized success plan and implementing strategies for growth and development, you can overcome obstacles, seize opportunities, and achieve your goals with confidence and purpose. Stay committed to your vision, stay resilient in the face of challenges, and never lose sight of the extraordinary potential that lies within you.

Conclusion

As we come to the end of this journey through the secrets of success, it's essential to reflect on the key insights and lessons learned along the way, find encouragement to take action toward our goals, and embrace the possibilities of the journey ahead.

RECAP OF KEY INSIGHTS AND LESSONS

Throughout this book, we've explored the habits, mindsets, and strategies of top achievers from various fields, uncovering the principles that underpin their success. From setting clear goals and cultivating a growth mindset to prioritizing well-being and nurturing meaningful relationships, we've seen how success is not merely about reaching a destination but about the journey of growth, learning, and self-discovery.

We've learned that success is not reserved for a select few but is attainable for anyone willing to put in the effort, discipline, and perseverance required to achieve their goals. By embracing failure as a stepping stone to success, staying resilient in the face of adversity, and continually seeking opportunities for growth and development, we can unlock our full potential and create a life of purpose, fulfillment, and impact.

Encouragement for Taking Action Towards Success

Now is the time to translate these insights into action and embark on your own journey toward success. Take inspiration from the stories of top achievers who have overcome obstacles, defied expectations, and achieved greatness against all odds. Use their examples as a source of motivation and encouragement as you pursue your dreams and aspirations.

Remember that success is not a destination but a continual process of growth and evolution. Celebrate your progress along the way, no matter how small, and remain steadfast in your commitment to your goals. Stay focused on what truly matters to you, and don't be afraid to take risks, make mistakes, and learn from failure.

Final Thoughts on the Journey Ahead

As you continue on your journey toward success, keep in mind that the path may not always be smooth or straightforward. There will be challenges, setbacks, and moments of doubt along the way. But it is precisely in those moments that your resilience, determination, and courage will be put to the test.

Embrace the journey with an open heart and an open mind, knowing that every experience – whether positive or negative – is an opportunity for growth and learning. Trust in yourself and your abilities, and have faith that you have everything you need to succeed within you.

Above all, remember that success is not defined by external accolades or material wealth but by the fulfillment and joy that come from living a life aligned with your values, passions, and purpose. Stay true to yourself, follow your heart, and never lose sight of the extraordinary potential that lies within you.

With courage, determination, and perseverance, you can achieve anything you set your mind to. The journey toward success begins with a single step – are you ready to take it?

References

1. Covey, S. R. (1989). *The 7 Habits of Highly Effective People: Powerful Lessons in Personal Change*. Free Press.

2. Dweck, C. S. (2006). *Mindset: The New Psychology of Success*. Ballantine Books.

3. Duckworth, A. (2016). *Grit: The Power of Passion and Perseverance*. Scribner.

4. Gladwell, M. (2008). *Outliers: The Story of Success*. Little, Brown and Company.

5. Hill, N. (1937). *Think and Grow Rich*. The Ralston Society.

6. Newport, C. (2016). *Deep Work: Rules for Focused Success in a Distracted World*. Grand Central Publishing.

7. Pink, D. H. (2009). *Drive: The Surprising Truth About What Motivates Us*. Riverhead Books.

8. Sinek, S. (2009). *Start with Why: How Great Leaders Inspire Everyone to Take Action*. Portfolio.

9. Duckworth, A., Peterson, C., Matthews, M. D., & Kelly, D. R. (2007). *Grit: Perseverance and passion for long-term goals*. Journal of personality and social psychology, 92(6), 1087–1101.

10. King, D. (2020). *Atomic Habits: An Easy & Proven Way to Build Good Habits & Break Bad Ones*. Avery.

11. Cain, S. (2012). *Quiet: The Power of Introverts in a World That Can't Stop Talking*. Crown Publishers.

12. Duhigg, C. (2012). *The Power of Habit: Why We Do What We Do in Life and Business*. Random House.

13. Kiyosaki, R. T. (1997). *Rich Dad Poor Dad: What the Rich Teach Their Kids About Money That the Poor and Middle Class Do Not*. Warner Books.

14. Duckworth, A. (2013). *True Grit: The Best Measure of Success and How to Teach It*. Scientific American.

15. Carnegie, D. (1936). *How to Win Friends and Influence People*. Simon and Schuster.

16. Csikszentmihalyi, M. (1990). *Flow: The Psychology of Optimal Experience*. Harper & Row.

17. Maxwell, J. C. (2007). *The 21 Irrefutable Laws of Leadership: Follow Them and People Will Follow You*. Thomas Nelson.

18. Clear, J. (2018). *Atomic Habits: An Easy & Proven Way to Build Good Habits & Break Bad Ones*. Avery.

19. Coyle, D. (2009). *The Talent Code: Greatness Isn't Born. It's Grown. Here's How*. Bantam Books.

20. Duckworth, A. (2016). *Grit: The Power of Passion and Perseverance*. Scribner.

www.ingramcontent.com/pod-product-compliance
Lightning Source LLC
Chambersburg PA
CBHW070415230526
45471CB00006B/2823